Family Guide

A Workbook Based on the Million-Copy Best-Seller

Preparing for Adolescence

*Helping Parents and Kids
Survive the Coming Years
of Change,
Together*

DR. JAMES DOBSON

Discussion Starters, Activities and Other Ideas to Help
Parents and Kids Talk Together About Important Issues

Regal Books

A Division of GL Publications
Ventura, California, U.S.A.

EDITORIAL STAFF

Mark Maddox, Publisher
Annette Parrish, Managing Editor
Carol Eide, Youth Editor
Billie Baptiste, Consulting Editor
Judith Roth, Assistant Editor
Hope Deck, Editorial Coordinator

WRITERS

Karen Linamen
Ed Stewart

DESIGN/ILLUSTRATION

Ted R. Killian, Senior Designer

Unless otherwise noted, Scripture quotations in this book are from the Holy Bible, *New International Version.* Copyright © 1973, 1978, 1984 International Bible Society. Used by permission of Zondervan Bible Publishers.

Also quoted is *The Everyday Bible, New Century Version,* copyright © 1987, 1988 by Word Publishing, Dallas, Texas 75039. Used by permission.

Published by Gospel Light Publications, Ventura, California 93006.

Contents

Preparing to Prepare for Adolescence

Dear Parent,

Your preteen or young teenager is embarking on quite a journey—and taking the entire family along for the ride, as well. You *can* help your son or daughter prepare for this exciting—and challenging—passage of life called adolescence.

A few of the things your child will need to know to survive this physical and emotional roller-coaster ride are:

- It's naturally a time of stress and agitation.

- The discomfort is almost universal. Even kids who seem entirely carefree feel uncomfortable at some time during adolescence.

- The best news of all is that adolescence has a predictable beginning *and* a predictable end. There is light at the end of the tunnel, folks!

What to say...

If you're like many adults, you're probably wondering just *what* you should say to your preteen to prepare him or her for the coming years—and of equal importance, *how* you should go about saying it.

Let's begin with the "what."

In his book, *Preparing for Adolescence*, Dr. Dobson gives an example of a football coach in the locker-room with his team, minutes before the kickoff of a big game. No coach in his right mind would miss taking the opportunity to provide last minute instruction and summarize the important things he's been teaching his players all along.

You are not unlike that coach. Whether you are a parent, stepparent, guardian, foster parent or teacher, as your young player heads out onto the field, it's time for a little pep talk; a time to reemphasize biblical values and give the last minute instructions your child will need to survive the pressures that will occur in the coming years.

And that's the whole purpose of this *Preparing for Adolescence Family Guide*: to help you summarize what your child needs to know about self-esteem, peer pressure, sexual development, emotional growth and independence, and a solid relationship with God.

How to say it...

This leads us to the next question: *how* to go about communicating these valuable principles.

It's a well-known phenomena that children and their parents are often suddenly transformed at the onset of puberty. Sometimes Junior may seem like a stranger. And from Junior's perspective, the word "parent" can be associated with a whole new set of adjectives—many of them less than complimentary!

The dynamics of these changes demand solid communication skills. And building them takes time. And commitment. And practice!

The 20 sessions in this book will require a total of about three and a half hours of your time. May I suggest that you plan these hours carefully. Good communication doesn't just "happen"—it takes effort.

But the effort pays off. As you practice a commitment to communication with your preteen, he or she will begin to develop vital skills needed later on in relationships with coworkers, friends, family and spouse. And you may very well find unexpected joy in developing a new person-to-person friendship with somebody who is no longer a child.

A few do's and don'ts.

As you begin to use this *Preparing for Adolescence Family Guide*, you'll want to remember these things:

1. DO work one-on-one. Including other siblings might hamper the effectiveness of each session. (In a group setting we suggest that you use the *Preparing for Adolescence Group Guide*. See information in the back of this book.)

2. DO plan your course with specific dates and times—but don't get too businesslike about it. Relax! Have fun!

3. DO feel free to share from your own experiences as an adolescent and teen. Relating the memories of your own adolescence with your preteen gives you credibility as a guide who's "been there" and knows the ropes. This credibility takes you and your child one step closer to an adult-to-adult relationship. And it enhances your empathy toward your preteen—putting you in touch with the many issues of adolescence. This does not mean that you have to communicate everything in your past, including areas over which you feel regret or inadequacy. You can be as general or specific as you choose about past problems. If you don't want to elaborate, don't.

4. DO commit to a time schedule which is convenient for both you and your preteen. Dr. Dobson suggests that you approach this time together with an attitude of expectation and excitement and that you involve your preteen in planning the event. Some ideas that have created a profitable experience for others include the following:

- A very effective plan is to schedule a one-time weekend getaway or retreat with your teen or preteen. Simply say, "Would you like to go on a special trip that will help to prepare you for becoming a man (or a woman)?"

- On a trip by car, you and your preteen can listen to the audiotapes of *Preparing for Adolescence* (see information in the back of this book) as you drive, then work through the *Family Guide* exercises at stops. You might plan a special fishing or sightseeing trip—even a one-day retreat at a local park can provide the perfect setting for a memorable time for you and your child.

You might also consider these options:

- Meet once or twice a week. There are 20 lessons and each should take about ten minutes, although some may last longer. You may also review two or more lessons at once. Between sessions you will need to read an average of eight pages of the book *Preparing for Adolescence* by Dr. James Dobson. You might want to encourage your preteen to read the book, as well, or listen together to the audiotapes covering the same material.

- Consider scheduling your sessions to coincide with a church youth group's study of the same material (see information about group material in the back of this book).

5. DON'T worry about what to do. Just stick with the program and follow directions as they come.

6. DON'T worry about seeing immediate "results." Your preteen will be realizing the full value of these sessions over a period of years. He or she will still make mistakes—perhaps glorious ones. But in the painful consequences of mistakes, the security of your love and the bonds of communication strengthened during these sessions will go a long way.

7. DON'T worry about having to be right all the time. Allow your child the precious knowledge that you are human, too, and that you may not always have the right answers.

It is best if your son or daughter reads the pages in *Preparing for Adolescence* (or you listen together to the segment of the audiotapes) that correspond with each *Family Guide* exercise ahead of time, although the guidebook can be effective alone, as well. You will want to read *Preparing for Adolescence* (or listen to the audiotapes) in advance of the time you will meet with your preteen. If you use the audiotapes, listen ahead of time to Parent Tapes I and II. These tapes contain additional background information that will help you use this material. You'll want to be prepared with pencils and paper for each session. Have a Bible handy for the sessions where it is used.

Think of this *Family Guide*, coupled with the book *Preparing for Adolescence,* as a road map and compass for the tumultuous and exciting journey just ahead. With the right preparation, the passage into adulthood can be a rewarding time of growth and discovery for your preadolescent—and for you, as well.

The Good News and Bad News About Growing Up*

> ● Read pages 13 through 16 in the paperback book *Preparing for Adolescence* by Dr. James Dobson (or listen to the corresponding segment of Side 1, Tape 1 from the *Family Tape Pack*—see information in the back of this book) before beginning this session.

Growing up will not be the easiest thing you'll ever do. It was not easy for those who are now adults, and you won't find it simple either. It's always difficult to grow up, because life presents many new demands when you enter a new phase.
Preparing for Adolescence, page 14

(What are some of the different phases of life?)
Dr. Dobson, in the book *Preparing for Adolescence,* talks about one stage of your life that you don't really remember: when you were curled, snug and cozy, inside your mother's body. It must have been a shock for you when—suddenly!—you were pushed out of your warm pocket and began confronting things you'd never experienced before: light; air; cold; colors—and touch and sound in ways you'd never imagined!

The journey from one period in life to the next—out of the womb and into the world—was filled with many new experiences. Some were scary and others were exciting, some were pleasant and some were not!

Experiencing a change from one stage of life to another might make it seem like the end of the world is at hand, but everyone, at every age goes through phases. Think about your parents and the first time they had a baby (that baby might have been you, or an older brother or sister). Becoming parents meant getting used to a great many changes—like changing diapers, sleeping less, wiping runny noses and discovering entire new levels of love for the little person who came to stay.

Beginning a new period in life is a rewarding part of growing and living.

But it can be work, too!

You're lucky to have a parent or adult who cares enough to prepare you well for the exciting years ahead. Together, you are about to learn some important things about . . . You!

> You can't stay in that childhood world forever, any more than you could remain in your mother's body. There's something better ahead for you—the excitement of growing up, of becoming an adult, of having your own family, of earning your own living, of making your own decisions. There will be some new fears and some new problems, and the world won't be quite as safe as it used to be. But it's an exciting world, and it will be even better if you know what to expect.
> *Preparing for Adolescence,* page 15

*A 10 to 15 minute parent/preteen workout which complements Session 1 in the *Preparing for Adolescence Group Guide*. For more information about the *Group Guide* see the back of this book.

The Activities

1. *Self-Portrait.* Let's look at a few of the pit-stops in your journey through life. Each of you draw three simple self-portraits, showing how you looked at the beginning of a phase you have experienced in life. Phases might include: being a newborn baby, starting school, learning to walk, getting married, beginning adolescence, having children, etc. These "maps" show you where you have traveled on your journey so far! Beneath each map write one bad thing and two good things about that stage of your life.

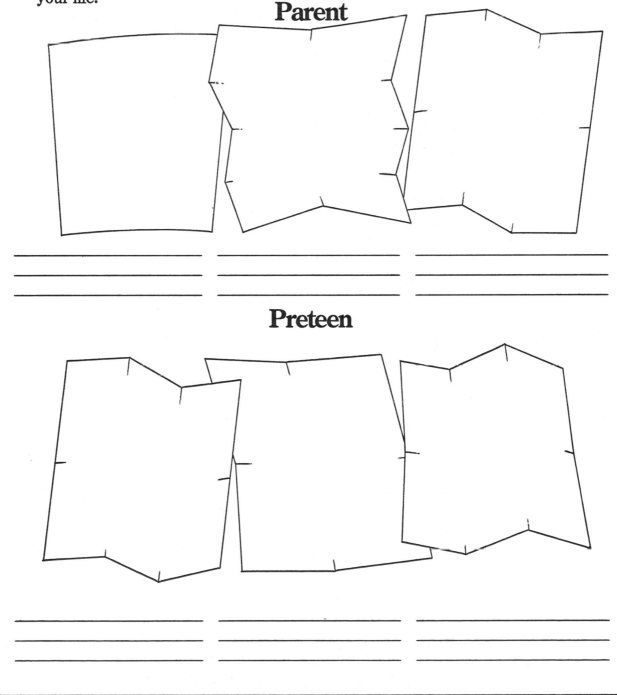

Parent

Preteen

2. *What Do You Think About Growing Up?* Brainstorm together the good news and bad news about being a child and being a teenager.

What's good about being a child?

A. _____

B. _____

C. _____

What's good about being a teenager?

A. _____

B. _____

C. _____

What's bad about being a child?

A. _____

B. _____

C. _____

What's bad about being a teenager?

A. _____

B. _____

C. _____

3. *Changeless in the Midst of Changes.* Read aloud Hebrews 13:8. What great news does this verse offer the Christian regarding changes ahead?

_____

_____

_____

4. *Prayer.* Thank God for His consistency and faithfulness. Pray that He will help you focus on the good news for the next several years of change and growth.

Everybody Gets Put Down Sometime. *Everybody!**

- Read pages 16 through 21 in the paperback book *Preparing for Adolescence* by Dr. James Dobson (or listen to the corresponding segment of Side 1, Tape 1 from the *Family Tape Pack*) before beginning this session.

- You'll need: A pocket calculator (optional).

> I want to warn you about a problem that lies down the road—a "canyon" that most teenagers fall into on the road to adulthood. This is not a problem that affects just a few teenagers; nearly everybody has to deal with it one way or another during the adolescent years.
> *Preparing for Adolescence*, page 17

It's hard to believe, but feelings of inferiority apply to everyone!

It doesn't always seem that way when you look around and see kids at school who appear to have it all together. It's hard to believe that beautiful Brianna or comedian John or stuck-up Sarah have moments when they feel unwanted and lonely.

Did you know that acting "stuck-up" and better than everyone else is really just one way of hiding how scared you feel inside?

Did you know that acting like the class clown is another way to deal with insecurity?

Did you know that the kids you think are pretty or handsome still come to school feeling clumsy and ugly—and worried sick about that pimple they're getting on the end of their nose?

> Some young people feel inferior and foolish only occasionally, such as when they fail at something very important. But others feel worthless all the time.
> *Preparing for Adolescence*, page 20

The point is, no one is immune. And just knowing that insecurity and inferiority strikes everyone can help a lot when you begin to feel down. It might even help you to take these feelings a little less seriously when they come. By being prepared—and knowing that your feelings aren't unique to you—you can avoid a lot of the damage to your self-esteem that often comes with the process of growing up.

> What a shame that most teenagers decide they are without much human worth when they're between thirteen and fifteen years of age! It may have happened to some of you even earlier, but in most cases the problem is at its worst during the junior high years.
> *Preparing for Adolescence*, page 18

*A 10 to 15 minute parent/preteen workout which complements Session 1 in the *Preparing for Adolescence Group Guide*.

The Activities

1. *Put-Down Poll.* Discuss how many times in a typical week somebody or something makes you feel inferior or put-down. Write your estimate of total put-downs in the box.

Average total put-downs we get weekly.

2. *Multiplication Mania.* Check each other's calculations on the following multiplication problem. Parent, you may only do the problem in your head. Son or daughter, you may jot figures below or use a calculator.

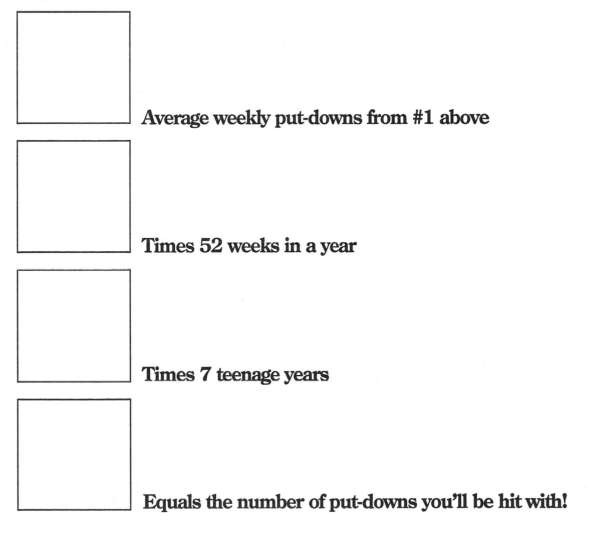

Average weekly put-downs from #1 above

Times 52 weeks in a year

Times 7 teenage years

Equals the number of put-downs you'll be hit with!

3. *Jump to a Conclusion.* Check what you both feel is the *best* conclusion about your mathematical findings.

☐ **The world** *really* **tries to make us feel inferior.**

☐ **Life will be easy on our egos.**

☐ **We'd better prepare for put-downs.**

☐ **Our mathematical skills are sad.**

☐ **Other:** _____

4. *One-on-One Survey.* Ask each other: "Why do you think teenagers are so good at putting down other people?"

_____
_____
_____
_____
_____

5. *Even Jesus?* Take turns reading verses about the Crucifixion scene in Matthew 27:39-44. Then read the following lines together:

Even perfect people feel put down sometimes!
　　Imagine Jesus saying to you, "When others make fun of you as a teenager or at any age, I know how you feel. They made fun of Me, and I'm the God of the universe!"
　　Jesus' response to put-downs? "Father, forgive them, for they do not know what they are doing" (Luke 23:34).

6. *Prayer.* Pray that, when people make fun of you, snub you, treat you like you don't matter, you'll forgive them as Jesus did—and that you won't believe what they say about you!

Looks Aren't Everything—Thank Goodness!*

- Read pages 21 through 23 in the book *Preparing for Adolescence* by Dr. James Dobson (or listen to the corresponding segment of Side 1, Tape 1 from the *Family Tape Pack*) before beginning this session.

- You'll need: Colored pencils or pens.

Did you know that about 80 percent of the teenagers in our society don't like the way they look? *Eighty percent!*

If you asked ten teenagers what they are most unhappy about, eight of them would be dissatisfied with some feature of their bodies....Most teenagers examine themselves carefully in the mirror to see how much damage has been done by Mother Nature, and they don't like what they see. Since none of us is perfect, they usually find something about themselves that they don't like.

Preparing for Adolescence, page 21,22

Why do we always have something about ourselves that we don't like?

Suzanne wants to be petite like Mary, while Mary could scream for blonde hair like Suzanne's.

Nancy wishes she were shorter; David wishes he were taller.

Mark longs for muscles like Michael's, but Michael is too busy mourning over his acne to enjoy the fact that he's the first in his class to begin developing a mature body!

I have an idea. Ask your parent if he or she grew up hating something about their bodies—there's an 80 percent chance that the answer is yes!

*A 10 to 15 minute parent/preteen workout which complements Session 2 in the *Preparing for Adolescence Group Guide*.

The Activities

1. *React to the Facts.* Read together:

> Dr. Dobson says that 80 percent of the teenagers in our society don't like the way they look.

Check the statement which summarizes your reaction to Dr. Dobson's comment:

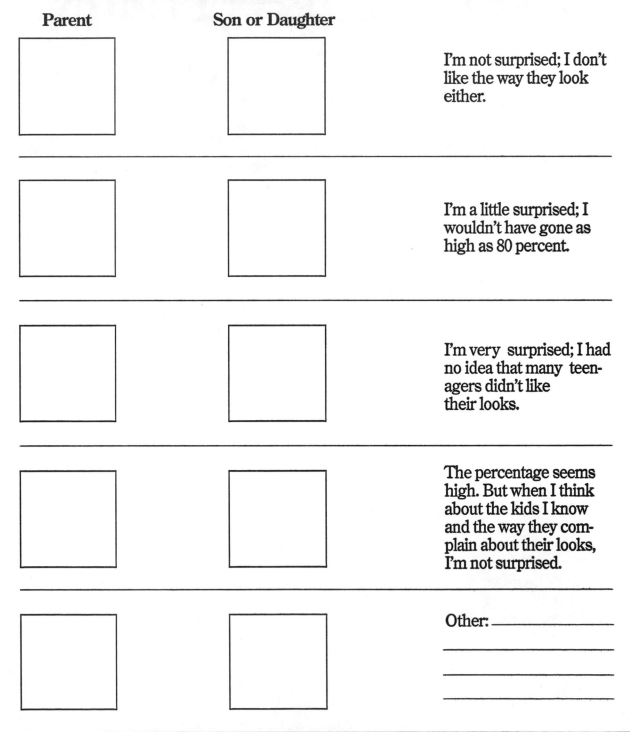

Parent   **Son or Daughter**

I'm not surprised; I don't like the way they look either.

I'm a little surprised; I wouldn't have gone as high as 80 percent.

I'm very surprised; I had no idea that many teenagers didn't like their looks.

The percentage seems high. But when I think about the kids I know and the way they complain about their looks, I'm not surprised.

Other: _____

_____

_____

_____

2. *Pinpointing the Problem.* Use the sketch below to identify what you think the 80-per-cent types don't like about their looks. Try to write at least one problem at the end of each arrow. Add more arrows if you can.

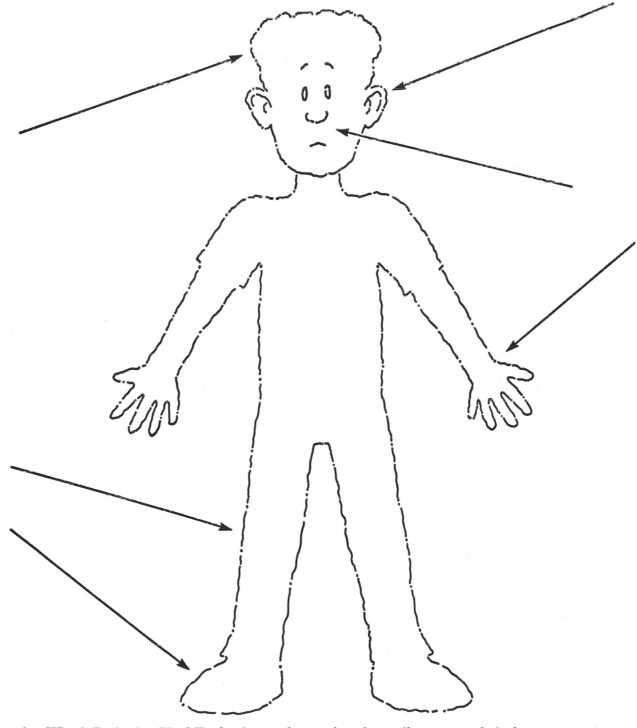

3. *What's Bothering You?* Each of you take a colored pencil or pen and circle one area on the sketch representing something about your looks which occasionally bothers you.

4. *The 20-Percent Club.* Here's a verse which could get you into the 20-Percent Club, those who are learning to accept their looks as God's gift to them. Unscramble each word to find out why you don't need to feel inferior about your looks.

I spreia uyo eescuba uoy

——— ———————— ———— —————— ————

dame em ni na zamagin dan

———— —— —— —— ————————— ———

flowdrune yaw. Thaw oyu

—————————— ———— . ———— ————

heav node si drewnufol.*

———— ———— —— ————————— .

5. *Prayer.* It may be difficult, but thank God for your looks, especially those things you can't change. Ask Him to help you develop your inner beauty and handsomeness.

* "I praise you because you made me in an amazing and wonderful way. What you have done is wonderful" (Ps. 139:14, *The Everyday Bible*).

Sticks and Stones Hurt—and So Do Nicknames!*

● Read pages 23 through 27 in *Preparing for Adolescence* by Dr. James Dobson (or listen to the corresponding segment of Side 2, Tape 1 from the *Family Tape Pack*) before beginning this session.

One of the most damaging games played by teenagers is to create unkind nicknames that draw attention to anything different or unusual about a person. In this way they put a spotlight on the feature that the victim most wants to hide. *Preparing for Adolescence,* page 23

Dr. Dobson talks about the three things that teenagers (and many adults!) feel they must have in order to feel good about themselves.

The top on the list is physical attractiveness.

The second value teens use to measure their worth is intelligence.

The third is money.

When a young person is lacking—even a very small lack!—in any of the three areas, it can invite ridicule from peers. Name-calling might appear harmless—unless you are the person who has just been dubbed with an unpleasant nickname! At that point you realize, firsthand, the awesome power that exists even in a single word.

Think about it. When God created the universe, all plant life, animals, light and water, what were His tools? There was no celestial contractor helping Him with the task; no divine bulldozers or heavenly hammer. God used something more powerful than tools made of iron—God used words.

Sometimes the words of peers, friends and family are painful. Even the people who love us most can unintentionally hurt us by what they say. But God has something for us, too, and His words contain healing and encouragement and hope!

Remember the TV commercial that goes, "When E.F. Hutton speaks, people listen!"?

Here is an even better idea. Let's listen to God's words.

*A 10 to 15 minute parent/preteen workout which complements Session 2 in the *Preparing for Adolescence Group Guide.*

The Activities

1. *What's in a Name?* One of you read aloud the paragraph headed "'Pee Wee' and 'Goril-la'" on page 23 of the book, *Preparing for Adolescence.*

2. *What's Your Handle?* The name tags below will help you think of some of the names and labels you are called. Fill them out.

Parent Name Tags   ### Preteen Name Tags

Hi, my name is...

_____
(your full name)

Hi, my name is...

_____
(your full name)

Hi, my name is...

_____
(a pet name your parents call[ed] you)

Hi, my name is...

_____
(a pet name your parents call you)

Hi, my name is...

_____
(a nickname you'd like)

Hi, my name is...

_____
(a nickname you'd like)

Hi, my name is...

_____
(a nickname or label which makes fun of you)

Hi, my name is...

_____
(a nickname or label which makes fun of you)

3. *Big Names.* God has many wonderful names and titles for those who belong to Him. How many can you think of from the Bible? Write them on the giant name tag below. Then each of you circle your favorite.

Hi, God calls me...

4. *Prayer.* Read the following prayer aloud together to God:

Dear Lord, thank You for never putting me down or making fun of me. Thank You for making me the way I am and for calling me

_____

_____

(your favorite names from #3)

Amen.

Toss Your Inferiorities to Jesus!*

> ● Read pages 29 through 36 in *Preparing for Adolescence* by Dr. James Dobson (or listen to the corresponding segment of Side 2, Tape 1 from the *Family Tape Pack*) before beginning this session.

> It will give you more confidence to know that everyone is afraid of embarrassment and ridicule—that we're all sitting in the same leaky boat, trying to plug the holes.
> *Preparing for Adolescence*, page 29

Recognizing that we aren't alone in our insecurities is one way to combat these feelings. But Dr. Dobson talks about some other ways, too.

He talks about listing the things about ourselves that make us feel anxious or inferior, then dividing all the things on that list into two groups:

1. Things that we can change.
2. And things that we can't!

It makes a lot of sense! Why should we spend a lot of time worrying about something we can't do anything about anyway? When we are anxious about our height, or whether our hair is too thick or too thin, or whether our nose is just the perfect shape, we're wasting energy that could be spent on things we could really do something about!

Okay. But now what do we do with the list of things we can't change? It's hard to just stop feeling concerned about things that seem so important.

Dr. Dobson suggests burning the list! He also suggests giving our problems to Jesus as we do it.

> Dear Jesus,
> I am bringing all my problems and worries to you tonight, because you are my best friend. You already know about my strengths and weaknesses, because you made me. That's why I'm burning this paper now. It's my way of saying that I'm giving my life

to you...with my good qualities along with my shortcomings and fail-
ures. I'm asking you to use me in whatever way you wish. Make me
the kind of person you want me to be. And from this moment for-
ward, I'm not going to worry about my imperfections.
Preparing for Adolescence, page 32

*A 10 to 15 minute parent/preteen workout which complements Session 3 in the *Preparing for Adolescence Group
Guide.*

The Activities

1. *Search for Good Advice.* The word search puzzle below contains 14 words which can be connected to form a statement that summarizes Dr. Dobson's good advice to those who feel inferior in any way. Work together to find the statement. The words may be vertical, horizontal, diagonal, upside down or backwards. Some words may share letters with other words. The solution to the puzzle is at the end of this session.

```
W  N  X  T  F  O  N  B  T  S  Q  Y
T  C  D  K  M  R  H  H  T  G  Z  U
I  C  B  N  W  K  A  P  H  N  V  Y
M  H  U  I  O  T  E  X  O  I  R  T
Z  A  V  K  W  C  P  M  S  H  T  Y
U  N  H  J  C  A  X  R  E  T  C  U
G  G  I  A  B  N  L  P  Q  A  A  O
A  E  I  O  T  N  R  A  E  L  M  Q
P  W  H  A  T  O  I  A  I  D  R  W
O  Y  N  A  C  T  C  H  A  N  G  E
O  O  B  M  B  R  T  I  Q  A  Y  U
C  T  E  C  H  A  N  G  E  D  E  S
```

Words used in puzzle:

AND	BE	CAN	CANNOT
CHANGE (2)	CHANGED	LEARN	THAT
THINGS	THOSE	TO	WHAT

2. *Hitting the Bull's-Eye.* What is something about you that you can change? What is something you cannot change but must learn to accept? Write one of these items in each bull's-eye.

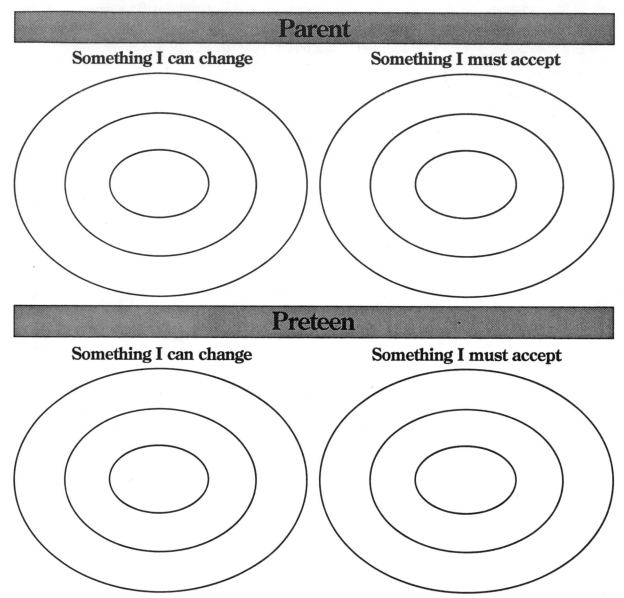

Parent

Something I can change   **Something I must accept**

Preteen

Something I can change   **Something I must accept**

3. *Disposable Problems.* First Peter 5:7 tells you what to do with your anxieties (things that bother you), including whatever makes you feel inferior. Read this verse together.

4. *Prayer.* Thank God that He cares for you and wants to take away your anxieties. Then give Him those items you have written on the bull's-eyes above. See the prayer on page 32 of Dr. Dobson's book, *Preparing for Adolescence,* for ideas on how to pray.

Solution to word search puzzle: Change what can be changed and learn to accept those things that cannot change.

Where's a Friend When You Need One?*

● Read pages 36 through 39 in *Preparing for Adolescence* by Dr. James Dobson (or listen to the corresponding segment of Side 2, Tape 1 from the *Family Tape Pack*) before beginning this session.

> You don't have to be beautiful or highly intelligent or wealthy in order to be liked by other people. "The best way to *have* a friend is to *be* a good friend to others." That's a very old proverb, but it's still very true.
> *Preparing for Adolescence*, page 36

Did you know that almost everyone is looking for a good friend?

You might have thought that you were the only one who gets lonely sometimes—but you're not. Everyone needs special friendships. They give us a chance to give and receive. We receive gifts of love, encouragement, constructive criticism and companionship. And we also have the privilege of giving these same things back to the special friends in our lives!

It's a two-way street.

If you're just looking for what you can get—if you're only looking for a friend who can give these gifts to you—you'll be looking a long time!

But if you are willing to reach out and make the first moves—give the first gifts—you'll never have to worry about not having enough friends!

Just one other question.

How do you choose the people who you want to be friends with? Do you look for the value that God created in every single man and woman, boy and girl? Or do you judge how much a person is worth by the standards you see in movies and on TV?

> The attributes that our society values most highly—beauty, intelligence and money—must be seen from the Christian point of view. These are *man's* values, but not *God's* values. The Lord doesn't measure your worth the way people do. He emphasizes

in His Word that each of us is worth more than the possessions of the *entire* world. This is true just because we are human beings....Those [other] factors don't make the difference at all.
Preparing for Adolescence, page 38

*A 10 to 15 minute parent/preteen workout which complements Session 3 in the *Preparing for Adolescence Group Guide*.

The Activities

1. *The Truth About Friends.* One of the following statements about the value of friends is true—the idea is right out of Dr. Dobson's book. The other statements are not true. Circle the true statement, then rewrite the others so that they are also true.

   The most important qualification for friends is that they have lots of money.

   True friendship is a one-way street.

   The best thing about friends is that you can get them to help you do your homework.

   Nothing helps your self-confidence more than genuine friends.

   Good friends are people who let you get into trouble if you want to.

2. *Emphasizing Friendship.* Take turns reading the following verse aloud, emphasizing a different boldfaced word each time:

   A friend loves you all the time. **A brother** is **always there** to **help you** (Prov. 17:17, *The Everyday Bible*, emphasis added).

3. *Speaking of Friends.* Fill in the bubbles in the cartoon strip below with a short conversation between two teenage friends who are building up each other's confidence according to Proverbs 17:17.

4. *Prayer.* If you have a Proverbs 17:17 friend, thank God for him or her. If not, ask God to help you find someone you can encourage and be encouraged by.

Is It OK to Be Like Everybody Else?*

- Read pages 41 through 52 in *Preparing for Adolescence* by Dr. James Dobson (or listen to the corresponding segment of Side 1 and the beginning of Side 2 of Tape 2 from the *Family Tape Pack*) before beginning this session.

- You'll need: An old junior high or high school yearbook belonging to your parent.

> This pressure to conform is so strong in some people that they feel uncomfortable if they are different in any way at all.
> *Preparing for Adolescence*, page 45

Did you know that doctors like to play tricks? Well, maybe not tricks exactly. They like to call it research.

Like the experiment where they invited ten teenagers into a room and showed them a series of cards, each with three straight lines printed on the face. One line was obviously shorter than all the rest, and the doctors asked the teenagers which was the shortest line.

It sounds pretty easy, huh?

Except that nine of the teens had been told to give the wrong answer. Nine teens looked at the card and agreed that the longest line was really the shortest!

Imagine how confused the one teen felt who didn't know that his friends were giving the wrong answer on purpose. He was probably wondering if they were all crazy, or if the crazy one was him.

So you know what he did? He voted with his friends. He said the longest line was the shortest, even though he knew that was wrong.

Sounds crazy? It's not. It's called *peer pressure*, and every day young people just like yourself find themselves making bad decisions just to go along with a crowd.

Sometimes the decisions don't hurt you too much—like being confused about the length of some line. But other times the decisions hurt a lot. Smoking can lead to cancer. Drinking can lead to accidents and is often the first step to using drugs. And premarital sex can lead to a lot of mixed-up feelings and heartaches—even terrible diseases (like syphilis, gonorrhea or even AIDS) not to mention *babies!* Sometimes bad decisions can even lead to death.

> If you have even *one friend* who will stand with you against the group, you probably will have more courage too. But when you're all by yourself, it's pretty difficult to take your stand alone.
> *Preparing for Adolescence*, page 47

*A 10 to 15 minute parent/preteen workout which complements Session 4 in the *Preparing for Adolescence Group Guide*.

The Activities

1. *What's Your Style?* Compare the styles and fads of the parent's teenage generation with today's teenage styles and fads. (It might be fun to look at some pictures in the parent's old yearbook!) Write or sketch something which fits each category.

Parent's Generation of Teenagers	Today's Teenagers
Most popular music group	
Most popular hairstyle (boys or girls)	
Most popular item of clothing (boys or girls)	
Most popular slang word for something good	
Most popular slang word for something bad	

2. *The Problem with Conformity.* One of you read aloud the two paragraphs under the heading "Think About the Problem" on page 50 of Dr. Dobson's book, *Preparing for Adolescence.* Brainstorm, then write below some wrong things that can happen when teenagers conform without thinking.

3. *From Conformation to Transformation.* Read Romans 12:1,2 aloud. Discuss the meaning of the words *conform* and *transform.* How can obeying these verses help a Christian overcome the dangers of conformity?

4. *Prayer.* Thank God that He can keep you from the problems often associated with conformity. Present yourself and your interests to Him and ask Him to renew your mind to conform with His plan for you.

It Takes Courage Not to Be a Jellyfish!*

● Read pages 52 through 61 in *Preparing for Adolescence* by Dr. James Dobson (or listen to the corresponding segment of Side 2, Tape 2 from the *Family Tape Pack*) before beginning this session.

It will be helpful for you to think about these issues *before* you face a crisis with your friends. Recognize the fact that they are under the same "peer" pressure that you feel. They're tempted to take drugs or smoke or drink for the same reason you are—simply because they're afraid to be different.
Preparing for Adolescence, page 52

Guts. For some reason, we tend to think of guts in terms of physical action.

I mean, Superman has guts, right? The hero in your favorite action-packed TV show has guts. Crocodile Dundee has guts, too.

If someone on the movie screen beats up the bad guys, crosses a war zone, saves a victim in distress, flies a plane into the heat of battle or emerges unscathed from a high-speed car chase—we think they have courage!

But sometimes having guts means no physical action at all! In fact, sometimes taking no physical action demands the greatest courage of all!

The Bible tells us that when Jesus was dying on the Cross, He could have called armies of angels to rescue Him. He could have launched an afternoon of action that people would have remembered for years to come! He could have taken the easy way out.

But He didn't. He took heart action instead. Heart action means doing the thing you know is right, even if it means doing nothing at all with your body!

Sometimes heart action is the best way to stand up to peer pressure. Decide in your heart ahead of time that you won't let your body act out dangerous suggestions from your friends. Your friends might think you're weak—but that's only because they can't see all the strength that you are flexing inside. It's an action of your heart—and that takes more guts than body-action any day!

Most teenagers respect a guy or girl who has the courage to be his own person, even when being teased. An individual with this kind of confidence often becomes a leader. He's not made of putty inside. Instead, he has the guts to stand up for what he knows is right.
Preparing for Adolescence, page 54

*A 10 to 15 minute parent/preteen workout which complements Session 4 in the *Preparing for Adolescence Group Guide.*

The Activities

1. *Fiddle with a Riddle.* Talk about this for 30 seconds: How is a teenager who does what everybody else does like a jellyfish? (If you need ideas, read the first paragraph under the heading "The Courage to Lead" on page 52 of *Preparing for Adolescence*.)

2. *A Sea Full of Courage.* Take turns sketching a few sea creatures which symbolize a teenager who has courage to stand against conformity. After each sketch, have the other person guess why that creature represents courage.

3. *Courage Spell-Out.* Take turns reading Joshua 1:6-9 aloud. Can you think of at least one word or phrase about courage suggested by these verses which begins with each of its seven letters? Try it!

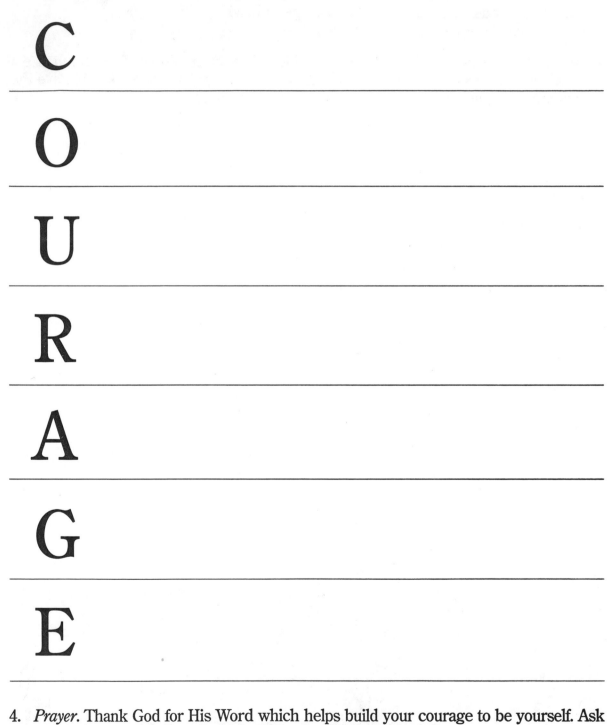

C _____

O _____

U _____

R _____

A _____

G _____

E _____

4. *Prayer.* Thank God for His Word which helps build your courage to be yourself. Ask Him to help you be strong and courageous to resist conformity.

What Time Is It on Your Puberty Clock?*

> ● Read pages 63 through 76 in *Preparing for Adolescence* by Dr. James Dobson (or listen to the corresponding segment of Side 1 and the beginning of Side 2 of Tape 3 from the *Family Tape Pack*) before beginning this session.

> This fantastic transformation reminds me in some ways of a caterpillar, which spins a cocoon around itself and then after a while comes out as a totally different creature—a butterfly.
> *Preparing for Adolescence*, page 65

There are many areas in life over which you have control. You have some control over what you eat, the friends you choose, your grades in school and how well you get along with siblings or parents.

But one area over which you have no control is the process called puberty. Dr. Dobson defines puberty as a sexual awakening in our bodies. It is the way our bodies equip themselves with the ability to produce children!

Puberty equals change. The shape of our bodies begins to change; hair begins to grow in new places; boys get lower voices and girls begin menstruation. These are just some of the many transformations that take place during puberty!

As you experience puberty, these changes may make you feel anxious at times.

Remember Session 5, where we talked about learning to accept the things we can't alter about ourselves? Puberty is one of those things. Rather than worrying about something you can't control, try to relax! Knowing what to expect will help a lot. It might also help to remember that when puberty begins, you are on your way to a grown-up body!

> These changes of puberty...may occur as early as nine or ten years of age or as late as seventeen or eighteen, but each boy and each girl has his or her own timetable.
> *Preparing for Adolescence*, page 74

*A 10 to 15 minute parent/preteen workout which complements Session 5 in the *Preparing for Adolescence Group Guide*.

The Activities

1. *How to Tell Time.* Changes in your body happen like clockwork during adolescence. But they don't always happen in predictable order. Parent, enter on the clock face below the "time" (age or year) at which some of these physical transformations happened to you. Son or daughter, check those changes which have already begun to occur in your body.

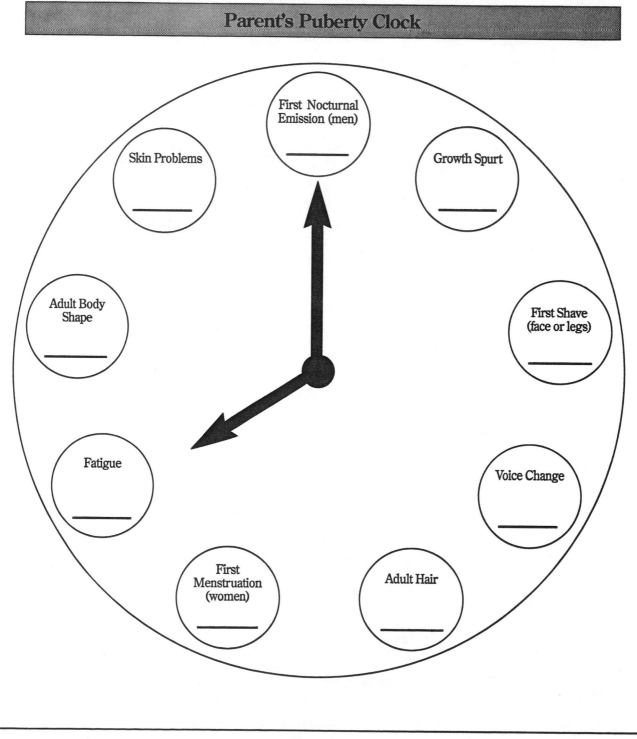

Parent's Puberty Clock

Preteen's Puberty Clock

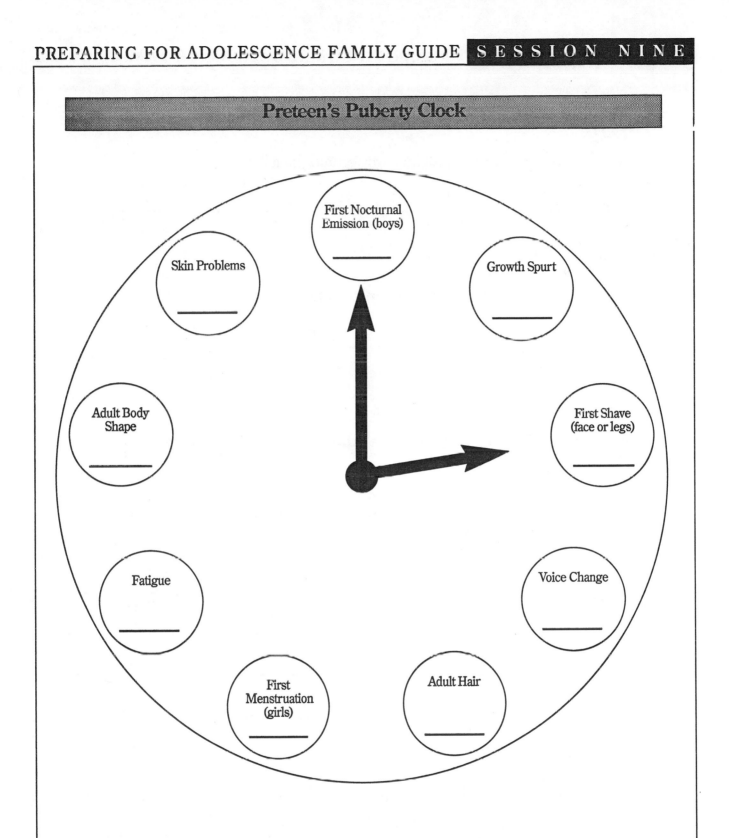

2. *Is Your Clock Running Fast or Slow?* Some puberty time clocks run faster than others. Is that a problem? Read aloud the first paragraph under the heading "The Bridge of Late Maturity" on page 74 of Dr. Dobson's book, *Preparing for Adolescence*.

3. *The Great Clockmaker in the Sky.* Take turns reading Psalm 139:13,14. Young person answer:

Who made your body with all its complicated parts?

_____

_____

Who set and wound your puberty time clock?

_____

_____

Do you think He can keep it ticking through all the changes ahead of you? Why or why not?

_____

_____

_____

_____

_____

_____

_____

_____

4. *Prayer.* Thank God for the amazing detail in the puberty time clock of your body. Ask Him to help you remain patient and thankful as you "ticktock" your way to full adulthood.

Sex Is Supposed to Be a Four-Letter Word: Pure*

> ● Read pages 76 through 86 in *Preparing for Adolescence* by Dr. James Dobson (or listen to the corresponding segment of Side 2, Tape 3 from the *Family Tape Pack*) before beginning this session.

Remember from Session 9, how puberty means your body is gearing up for the grown-up process of producing children? Just as your body undergoes a physical transformation so that child-bearing can become a reality in the years ahead, you begin to change in other ways as well.

In his book *Preparing for Adolescence*, Dr. Dobson points out that the desire for sex was God's idea, not man's. God knows that it takes more than a grown-up body to produce children and families. It takes grown-up desires, too! That's why, somewhere between your twelfth and fifteenth birthdays, you will begin to develop new desires and cravings that involve the matter called sex.

> Boys will become very interested in the bodies of girls—in the way they're built, in their curves and softness, and in their pretty hair and eyes....If you're a boy, it's very likely that you will think often about these fascinating creatures called girls, whom you used to hate so much!
>
> Girls, on the other hand, will not be quite so excited over the shape and the look of a boy's body (although they will find them interesting). They will be more fascinated by the boy himself—the way he talks, the way he walks, the way he thinks.
> *Preparing for Adolescence*, page 77

These new attractions are exciting and good, and are part of God's plan for your sexuality!

Understanding these new feelings—and that they are meant to lead you into a successful and happy marriage relationship—can help you when you are faced with opportunities to follow your new feelings into dangerous situations. God created marriage as the perfect place for us to practice—and even protect!—the wonderful gift of sex.

If someone gave you a perfect rose with velvet-soft petals, would you stuff it in your locker at school? Would you carry it onto the basketball court during gym? Would you wag it out of the window of the school bus on your way home? Of course not. The only place for a rose to survive and thrive is in the safety of a vase, nurtured by water.

Sex outside of marriage can leave you feeling pretty battered, crushed and torn. But in the safety of marriage, nurtured by the love between a husband and wife, it's a beautiful gift from God.

*A 10 to 15 minute parent/preteen workout which complements Session 5 in the *Preparing for Adolescence Group Guide*.

The Activities

1. *Scrambled Clues.* Unscramble these three words to discover another major tick on the puberty clock.

T R E I T S E N   N I   E X S

_____ _____ _____

2. *A God-Given Hunger.* Take turns reading the first two paragraphs under the heading "The Sex Appetite" on pages 76 and 77 of Dr. Dobson's book, *Preparing for Adolescence.*

3. *Your Story in Pictures.* Parent, draw a simple cartoon strip, including captions, showing how you were first attracted to your child's other parent. Daughter or son, draw a cartoon strip illustrating when you first noticed that the opposite sex was attractive to you.

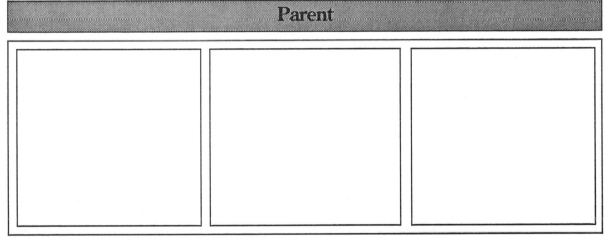

Parent

Daughter or Son

4. *What's the Problem?* Take turns answering these questions:

Why is it difficult for teenagers to wait to have sex until marriage?

_____   _____
_____   _____
_____   _____
_____   _____
_____   _____

Why should a teenager avoid premarital sex?

_____   _____
_____   _____
_____   _____
_____   _____
_____   _____
_____   _____

What can help a teenager resist the temptation to have sex?

_____   _____
_____   _____
_____   _____
_____   _____
_____   _____

5. *Prayer.* Thank God for His plan for sexuality. Ask Him for strength to avoid premarital sex.

What Is This Crazy Thing Called Love?*

- Read pages 87 through 94 in *Preparing for Adolescence* by Dr. James Dobson (or listen to the corresponding segment of Side 1, Tape 4 from the *Family Tape Pack*) before beginning this session.

- You'll need: A radio.

What changes take place in the minds of men and women who have fallen in love? How can they know when that love is genuine? Can they be fooled, thinking they are "in love" when they aren't? What is necessary to keep their love alive?
Preparing for Adolescence, page 87

"I loved that movie!"
"I sure love pizza. Don't you?"
"He's in love with that car!"
"I'd love another piece of chocolate!"
"I think I'm falling in love with you."

For a short, simple word, love can sure have a lot of different meanings! In the years just ahead, you will be dating and learning more about that short but very complex word, love. But before you dive right in, now is a good time to think about the different meanings—and different levels—of love.

Approximately *50 percent* of all teenage marriages end in divorce *within the first few years!* What a tragically high percentage! It means that *half* of all the people who thought they were "in love"—those who were tremendously excited with each other—quickly became disillusioned, bitter, unhappy, and broken....How do all these people get misled?
Preparing for Adolescence, page 90

Without a solid understanding of what love is—and isn't—you run the risk of making the same grave mistake that many young people have made. They make this mistake when they confuse one level of love for another!

It's fairly easy to do. Which is why this session and the ones following are so important. As you pioneer new territory with your heart, it's comforting to have some guidelines to keep you from getting lost!

*A 10 to 15 minute parent/preteen workout which complements Session 6 in the *Preparing for Adolescence Group Guide*.

The Activities

1. *Love According to the Top 40.* Spend 3-5 minutes spinning the dial on an AM or FM radio searching for love songs. Listen to each song you find long enough to discover what it is saying about love (30-60 seconds maximum). Then jot down a phrase about love from each song. **Warning:** Many songs on the radio today are filled with obscene and very objectionable language. Plan to preview the stations you will listen to and be sure to do this exercise *together* with your son or daughter.

LOVE IS...

_____

_____

_____

_____

_____

2. *The Great Love Failure.* Fill in the blanks in Dr. Dobson's statement using the words listed below. (Beware: Some of the words don't belong in the statement!) If you need help, the statement is found at the bottom of page 87 in *Preparing for Adolescence.*

Dr. Dobson says: "It is my belief that the high divorce _____ in our country results, in part, from the _____ of newlyweds to _____ what _____ is, what it is not, and how to make sense out of their _____."

UNDERSTAND	BATHTUB	RATE	EMOTIONS
EMOTIONS	LOVE	CAMEL	FAILURE

3. *Tuning into the Word.* What if 1 Corinthians 13:4-7 was a love song on the radio? Tune into these verses in your Bible and summarize what they say about love.

LOVE IS...

_____

_____

_____

_____

_____

_____

_____

_____

_____

_____

_____

_____

_____

_____

_____

4. *Prayer.* Thank God that He can help you understand what real love is, because He created it. Ask Him to cleanse your heart from false love and fill you with His love.

Puppy Love Only Works for Puppies*

● Read pages 94 through 101 in *Preparing for Adolescence* by Dr. James Dobson (or listen to the corresponding segment at the end of Side 1 and the beginning of Side 2 of Tape 4 from the *Family Tape Pack*) before beginning this session.

> That exciting feeling between two new "lovers" *never* continues for life. It can't last, simply because human emotions are constantly changing. Even when people *genuinely* love each other, there are times of great closeness, times when they feel nothing for each other, and times when they are irritable and grumpy.
> *Preparing for Adolescence*, page 97

Do these words surprise you? Maybe they even disappoint you. That might be because you're confusing real love with puppy love.

Puppy love feels great. All the time. It's a top-of-the-world feeling that makes everyone and everything else seem to disappear from your life! When you are in puppy love, the only thing that seems to matter is that one special person and how he or she makes you feel. When the feeling of puppy love begins to fade away, then puppy love goes right along with it.

But real love isn't a feeling. It's a promise to "be there" for your special someone even as the feelings come and go and come again.

There's nothing wrong with puppy love. It's just another part of your growth as you continue your journey toward adulthood. In fact, puppy love can be a lot of fun!—just as long as you realize what it is, and learn to separate real love from falling in love with a feeling.

*A 10 to 15 minute parent/preteen workout which complements Session 6 in the *Preparing for Adolescence Group Guide*.

The Activities

1. *Words to the Wise.* Fill in the missing letters to reveal two different kinds of love that Dr. Dobson talks about.

IT ( )S A

FEELI( )G WHICH

IS ( )LEETING AND

TEMPOR( )RY. IT IS

AN EMO( )ION WHICH

HAS ITS ( )PS AND DOWNS,

AND WHICH COMES ( )ND GOES

WI( )H CIRCUMSTANCES.

IT ( )S

( )NLY INTERESTED

IN WHAT BRI( )GS ME PLEASURE.

I( ) IS A

PE( )MANENT COMMITMENT

WHICH IS ( )NAFFECTED BY THE

ROLLER COAST( )R RIDE OF EMOTIONS.

IT IS ON( )Y INTERESTED IN

HON( )RING THE OTHER

PERSON AND GI( )ING TO MEET

HIS OR H( )R NEEDS.

2. *True Confession.* Parent, tell about some of your youthful experiences with puppy love and compare them to your experiences with genuine love. Son or daughter, have you experienced puppy love for someone yet? How did it make you feel?

3. *The Supreme* Test. Someone read aloud the two paragraphs under the heading "What's the Difference?" on pages 98, 99 of *Preparing for Adolescence.* Sketch something below which represents the important test which will help you determine one kind of love from the other.

4. *Roughly Translated.* The first three words of 1 Corinthians 13:8 are: "Love never fails." How many other ways can you say that phrase to express what it means?

Love is...

_____

_____

_____

Love is...

_____

_____

_____

Love is...

_____

_____

_____

Love is...

_____

_____

_____

Love is...

_____

_____

_____

_____

_____

5. *Prayer.* Thank God for loving you with genuine, selfless love. Ask Him to help you base all your relationships on His love.

Before You Say "I Do"*

> ● Read pages 101 through 105 and 116 through 118 in *Preparing for Adolescence* by Dr. James Dobson (or listen to the corresponding segments of Side 2, Tape 4 from the *Family Tape Pack*) before beginning this session.
>
> ● You'll need: A Bible.

It is possible, in my opinion, to love Jesus and be a good Christian, yet make a hasty decision to marry the wrong person.
Preparing for Adolescence, page 102

There's nothing wrong with dreaming about marriage, and about the kind of special person you would like to share your life with!

The problem is that many young people fuel their dreams with ideas that simply are not true. These young people head toward marriage filled with expectations that are far from reality.

Some of the false ideas that people have about marriage are listed below:
- People who really love each other never fight.
- It's better to marry the wrong person than to be single and lonely.
- God has one special person for me to marry, and He will guide us together.
- It's OK to have sex before marriage if two people really love each other.

The best way to get rid of false ideas is to replace them with truth. God's Word, the Bible, is one of the best sources of truth there is! That's why this session takes a look at some Bible verses dealing with love and marriage.

So go ahead and dream about the future—but let your dreams reflect what *God* says about the important topic of love.

*A 10 to 15 minute parent/preteen workout which complements Session 7 in the *Preparing for Adolescence Group Guide*.

The Activities

1. *Let's Get Real!* Preteen, take a moment to write down all the ideal traits that many young people are looking for in a boyfriend or girlfriend. Think about the features that are important to your friends, and even the kinds of characteristics that romantic movies and TV shows seem to make a big deal about. After you're done, pretend you are a big-time talk show host and interview your parent. Your parent has firsthand experience at the many challenges of real-life love. Find out what traits are *really* most valuable in a long-term relationship. Ask your parent if he or she had any unrealistic ideals going into marriage. Ask what advice your parent might give to the millions of teenage viewers who watch your show.

Popular Thoughts About Love and Marriage
(Preteen, write your collection of thoughts here)

_____

_____

_____

_____

_____

_____

_____

_____

_____

_____

_____

_____

_____

_____

_____

Words of Insight from a Veteran
(Take notes from the interview with your "TV guest" and write them here)

_____

_____

_____

_____

_____

_____

_____

_____

_____

_____

_____

_____

_____

_____

_____

_____

_____

_____

_____

2. *For Richer, For Poorer.* Read Ephesians 5:21-28. Imagine that your pastor is writing vows for your wedding. Based on these verses what are some promises which you should make to your future spouse?

I promise...

_____
_____
_____
_____

I promise...

_____
_____
_____
_____

I promise...

_____
_____
_____
_____

I promise...

_____
_____
_____
_____

I promise...

_____
_____
_____
_____

3. *Prayer.* Ask God to begin preparing you for the person you will marry. Thank Him in advance for His provision of a future godly mate and marriage.

The Good News About Saving Yourself Until Marriage*

● Read pages 105 through 116 in *Preparing for Adolescence* by Dr. James Dobson (or listen to the corresponding segment of Side 2, Tape 4 from the *Family Tape Pack*) before beginning this session.

> Sexual relationships during the teen years very rarely last.
> Less than 10 percent result in marriage, and about 50 percent
> of those who do marry divorce within five years. Most of the
> time, the relationships break up after a few weeks or months,
> leaving one or two heartbroken young people.
> *Preparing for Adolescence*, page 113

There are three consequences of having sex before marriage: sexually transmitted diseases, unplanned pregnancies and strong emotional attachments that can hinder future relationships, including your future relationship with a husband or wife!

That's the bad news.

The good news is that you don't have to experience any of these things.

> Saying no to sex when you are young and unprepared for the
> consequences can be a way of saying "I love you." I urge you to
> be strong in this area for yourself and for your friends.
> *Preparing for Adolescence*, page 113

Remember Session 7 where we talked about the problem with conformity? Here is one of the areas where you will have many opportunities to be a leader instead of a follower. Decide now what your answer will be when you are with a special person you like a lot, and are faced with an important choice about saving yourself sexually until you are married.

*A 10 to 15 minute parent/preteen workout which complements Session 7 in the *Preparing for Adolescence Group Guide.*

The Activities

1. *Heart-to-Heart Talk.* Discuss the following questions together:

   Do you know a Christian who has experimented with premarital sex? If so, how do you think he/she feels now about his/her premarital involvement?

   Do you know someone who has contracted a sexually transmitted disease (STD) through promiscuous sexual activity? If so, how do you think he/she feels now about his/her sexual behavior?

2. *No Aid for AIDS.* Create a billboard you would like to see outside your school informing young people about the dangers of AIDS and other STDs in our society.

3. *Now for the Good News.* Settle back and read aloud the section headed "Sexually Trans-mitted Diseases" on pages 109,110 of *Preparing for Adolescence.*

4. *Lifetime Guarantee.* Hebrews 13:4 states, "Marriage should be honored by all, and the marriage bed kept pure, for God will judge...all the sexually immoral." Fill in the guarantee form below based on this verse and what you have just read in Dr. Dobson's book.

Good News Guarantee

_____
(your name)

*is hereby guaranteed a lifetime
of freedom from sexually
transmitted diseases if he/she
follows these guidelines:*

_____

_____

_____

_____

_____

_____

_____

5. *Prayer.* Thank God for the protection He has provided for you in sexual purity. Ask God to help you stand strong against the sexual temptations you will face in the years ahead.

Adolescence Has Its Ups and Downs*

● Read pages 119 through 125 in *Preparing for Adolescence* by Dr. James Dobson (or listen to the corresponding segment of Side 1, Tape 5 from the *Family Tape Pack*) before beginning this session.

> Little things that won't bother you later in life will bug you as a teenager. Your fears will be more frightening, your pleasures will be more exciting, your irritations will be more distressing, and your frustrations will be more intolerable. Every experience will appear king-sized during adolescence. That's why teenagers are often so explosive, why they sometimes do things without thinking and then regret their behavior later. You'll soon learn that feelings run deep and powerful during the adolescent years.
> *Preparing for Adolescence,* page 124

It would sure be wonderful to feel great all of the time!
Or would it?
Contrasts, or opposites, are an important part of our everyday life. Without them, life would get pretty boring. We would also begin to take a lot of things for granted—like, for example, spring. The first warm days of spring bring songs to our hearts because of the cold, dark days of winter. If we never had a winter, spring wouldn't be nearly as exciting!

During your teen years, you will experience great opposites in the arena of your emotions. More than at any other point in your journey through time, during the teen years your emotions will take you for the ride of your life!

> When you're emotionally high, expect to come down; when you're rock bottom, expect to come up....Another way to describe these unstable feelings is to say that human emotions

are *cyclical*. They occur in regular patterns and are influenced by the amount of sleep you've had, what kind of health you're in, and how things are going in your life.
Preparing for Adolescence, page 125

*A 10 to 15 minute parent/preteen workout which complements Session 8 in the *Preparing for Adolescence Group Guide*.

The Activities

1. *Riding the Roller Coaster.* A teenager's feelings are like the highs and lows of a roller coaster ride. Brainstorm together several different emotions teenagers experience (highs, lows and in between) and write them along the track of the roller coaster below.

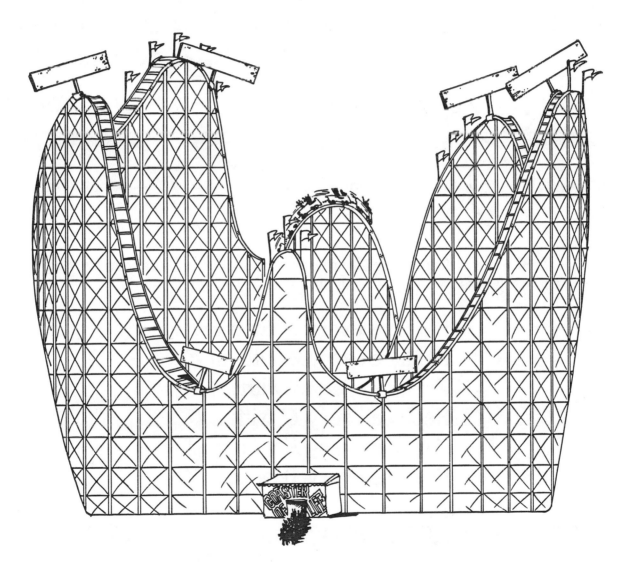

2. *Parent on the Spot.* Select two or three feelings from those on the roller coaster track. Ask your parent to tell you about a personal experience with each feeling from his/her adolescent years.

3. *Facing Your Feelings.* Fill in the faces below with expressions showing some of your main emotions. Then select a percentage for each face which shows about how often you feel that way.

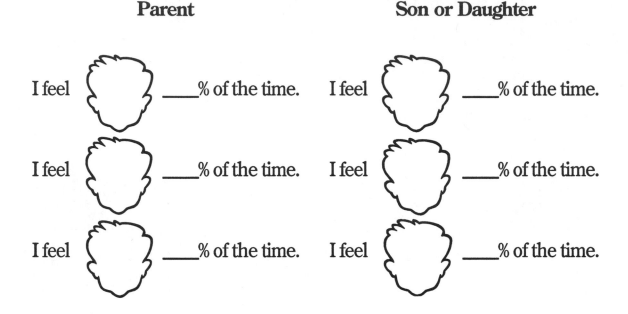

Parent		**Son or Daughter**	
I feel ____% of the time.		I feel ____% of the time.	
I feel ____% of the time.		I feel ____% of the time.	
I feel ____% of the time.		I feel ____% of the time.	

4. *Your Secret Strength.* Decode the following verse to discover God's strength to help you endure the ups and downs of your emotions.

Replace every *A* with a *T*.
Replace every *Z* with an *E*.
Replace every *X* with an *O*.
Replace every *Q* with a *U*.
Replace every *K* with an *I*.
Replace every *W* with a *Y*.

"AHZ JXW XF AHZ LXRD KS WXQR SARZNGAH" (Neh. 8:10).

____ ____ __ ____ ____ __ _____ _____

5. *Prayer.* Thank God for the stability He can bring in the midst of your changing emotions. Ask Him to help you focus on His strength through the emotional challenges of your teenage years.

Where There's God's Will, There's a Way*

● Read pages 125 through 127 in *Preparing for Adolescence* by Dr. James Dobson (or listen to the corresponding segment of Side 1, Tape 5 from the *Family Tape Pack*) before beginning this session.

You may have impressions of many kinds, and if you believe them to be true, they can cause you to make wrong decisions. Some impressions might lead you to get married suddenly, or move to another town, or quit school, or join the Army. When these strong thoughts and feelings come, just remember that God rarely makes demands that require instant change. Give yourself a few days or weeks to look at all sides of the issue. And the more important the decision, the more carefully you should review the facts.
Preparing for Adolescence, page 125,126

Everyone experiences these kinds of impressions or impulses. When they come, how do you know if they are just part of your imagination or emotions—or if God is telling you what to do?

Learning how to separate God's will from your own impressions is part of the process of maturing into an adult. You will make mistakes now and then, just because you're human and no one is immune from messing up! The goal is not "to be perfect and make no mistakes" (because that goal would be unreachable!), but to learn something each time we make a wrong decision so we can make a better decision next time!

There is no foolproof way to avoid following impressions instead of God's will. But the first activity lists five suggestions will help you know how to begin.

*A 10 to 15 minute parent/preteen workout which complements Session 8 in the *Preparing for Adolescence Group Guide*.

The Activities

1. *How to Know God's Will.* Draw a line from each of Dr. Dobson's suggestions for knowing God's will to the Bible verse that best applies.

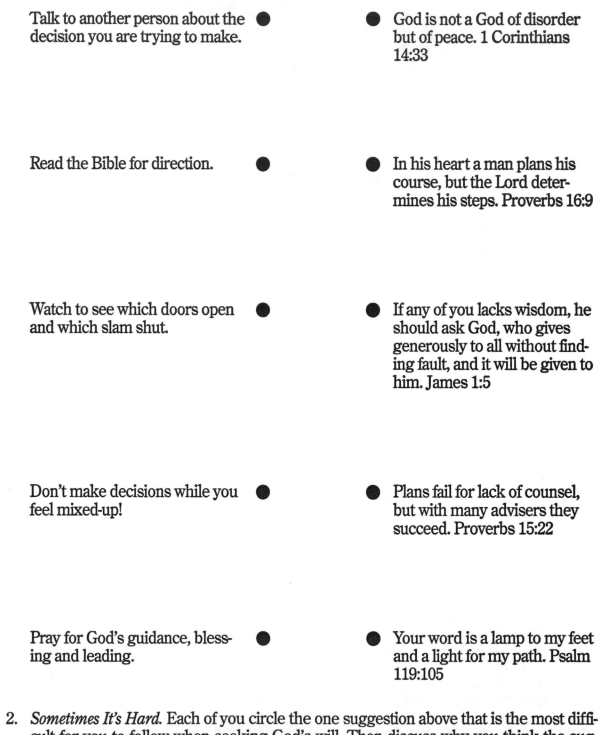

Talk to another person about the decision you are trying to make. ●

● God is not a God of disorder but of peace. 1 Corinthians 14:33

Read the Bible for direction. ●

● In his heart a man plans his course, but the Lord determines his steps. Proverbs 16:9

Watch to see which doors open and which slam shut. ●

● If any of you lacks wisdom, he should ask God, who gives generously to all without finding fault, and it will be given to him. James 1:5

Don't make decisions while you feel mixed-up! ●

● Plans fail for lack of counsel, but with many advisers they succeed. Proverbs 15:22

Pray for God's guidance, blessing and leading. ●

● Your word is a lamp to my feet and a light for my path. Psalm 119:105

2. *Sometimes It's Hard.* Each of you circle the one suggestion above that is the most difficult for you to follow when seeking God's will. Then discuss why you think the suggestion you circled is difficult for you.

3. *Thanks for the Memory.* Memorize Proverbs 3:5,6 by using the stage-by-stage strategy below.

   Photocopy this page. Then, fold each stage to the back after each of you can recite it. (Or, you could copy the verses, including blank lines where words have been omitted, onto three index cards or scraps of paper.)

"Trust in the Lord with all your heart and lean not on your own understanding; in all your ways acknowledge him, and he will make your paths straight" (Prov. 3:5,6).

"Trust in the ____ with all your heart and ____ not on your own _____; in all your ____ acknowledge him, and ____ will make your paths _____."

"Trust in the ____ with ____ your ____ and ____ not on ____ own _____; in ____ your ____ _____ him, and ____ ____ make your ____ _____."

"____ in the ____ with ____ ____ ____ and ____ ____ on ____ own _____; __ ___ your ____ _____ ____, and ____ ____ ____ your ____ _____."

4. *Prayer.* Thank God for His promise of guidance. Ask Him to help you implement Dr. Dobson's five suggestions in seeking God's will for your life.

Your Parents Brought You Up; Don't Let Them Down*

● Read pages 127 through 132 in *Preparing for Adolescence* by Dr. James Dobson (or listen to the corresponding segment at the end of Side 1 and the beginning of Side 2 of Tape 5 from the *Family Tape Pack*) before beginning this session.

● You'll need: A Bible.

> You had better prepare yourself for it: you will soon be your own boss....What I'm saying is that childhood begins with great dependence at birth and moves toward total independence at the far end of adolescence. During the same time, your parents are changing from servants to free people again. That's what childhood and adolescence and parenthood are all about.
> *Preparing for Adolescence*, page 128

Independence sounds great, doesn't it? For many young people in their adolescent years, their new-found purpose in life seems to be to become as independent as possible, as quickly as possible.

But independence never arrives unescorted. It always comes accompanied by another three-dollar word: responsibilities.

> If a person is not yet ready to accept all the responsibilities of living, then he is not ready to handle unrestricted freedom either.
> *Preparing for Adolescence*, page 130

If you want to prove to your parents that you are ready for more freedom, tell them you are ready to handle the additional responsibility that comes hand in hand. Parents will respond better to a show of maturity than a display of demands!

Nevertheless, there will still be times when you and your parents disagree on the amount of independence you are really ready to handle! When this happens, remember that these struggles are a natural part of the process of growing up and away from parental control. As you adjust to additional freedom, your parents are going through big adjustments, too, as they learn to release you bit by bit.

*A 10 to 15 minute parent/preteen workout which complements Session 9 in the *Preparing for Adolescence Group Guide.*

The Activities

1. *Independent Reading.* Take turns reading aloud the two sections headed "The Declaration of Independence" and "Completely Free" on pages 127-131 in *Preparing for Adolescence.*

2. *Keeping Your Balance.* Preteen, fill in the privileges you would like to enjoy in the years ahead. Parent, fill in the responsibilities which will qualify your child for the privileges he/she seeks. Complete the chart in pencil so you can alter the privileges and responsibilities if necessary as you discuss them.

	Ages 13-14	Ages 15-16	Ages 17-19
Privileges Desired			
Responsibilities Expected			

3. *The Way It Was.* Parent, tell about one incident from your teenage years when you and your parents were out of balance on your privileges and responsibilities.

4. *Balancing Your Accessories.* Proverbs 1:8,9 compares respect for parental instruction to the decorative accessories of a wardrobe. Read these verses, then summarize the message in your own words.

_____

_____

_____

_____

_____

_____

_____

_____

_____

_____

_____

_____

_____

_____

_____

_____

_____

_____

_____

_____

_____

_____

5. *Prayer.* Together, ask God for His guidance as you work on balancing privileges and responsibilities in your relationship at home. Thank Him for the harmony He can bring through the process.

The *R* Word.*

- Read pages 132 through 136 in *Preparing for Adolescence* by Dr. James Dobson (or listen to the corresponding segment of Side 2, Tape 5 from the *Family Tape Pack*) before beginning this session.
- You'll need: Game pieces (see Activity 1).

> As you progress through adolescence...it will be natural to examine each of the beliefs you have been taught. There will probably come a time when you will say, "Hey! Wait a minute. Do I really accept what my parents have said? Can I trust them to tell me the truth?"
> *Preparing for Adolescence,* page 135

During adolescence, you may experience times of conflict with your parents. You may also entertain new insights that maybe—just maybe—your parents don't know everything after all! Finally, there will very likely be times when you feel embarrassed to have your peers catch a glimpse of you in the presence of your parents.

About the matter of embarrassment in the presence of parents, Dr. Dobson has these encouraging words: "It's not because you don't love them; you shouldn't feel guilty about that. It's because you want to grow up and you're worried about peer pressure. It's all a normal part of the adolescent experience."

What a relief to know that all of these rather unsettling new feelings are a normal part of the great transition called adolescence.

But in the middle of all these expected, normal twists in your relationship with your parents, there is one temptation that you need to avoid! It may be tempting to express some of your new feelings with disrespect. Up until now, you have very likely been taught not to disagree with your folks. Now, facing sudden new urges to confront and test some of your parents' values and rules, you may not know how to disagree in a way that's constructive!

This is a good chance for you to learn how to express your disagreement—in an agreeable way! The following game will help you understand how you can stay respectful, practice good communication skills, and still express your feelings on sensitive topics!

*A 10 to 15 minute parent/preteen workout which complements Session 9 in the *Preparing for Adolescence Group Guide*.

The Activities

1. *What Can I Say?* Use the simple game below to help you practice respectful conversation.
   - Each select a game marker (coin, ring, paper clip, etc.). Place your marker on START.
   - Flip a coin to move. Heads, move two spaces; tails, move one space.
   - When you land on a space, respond to the situation by speaking respectfully to the other person for 10-20 seconds. If you land on a space already discussed, move to the next space which has not been discussed.

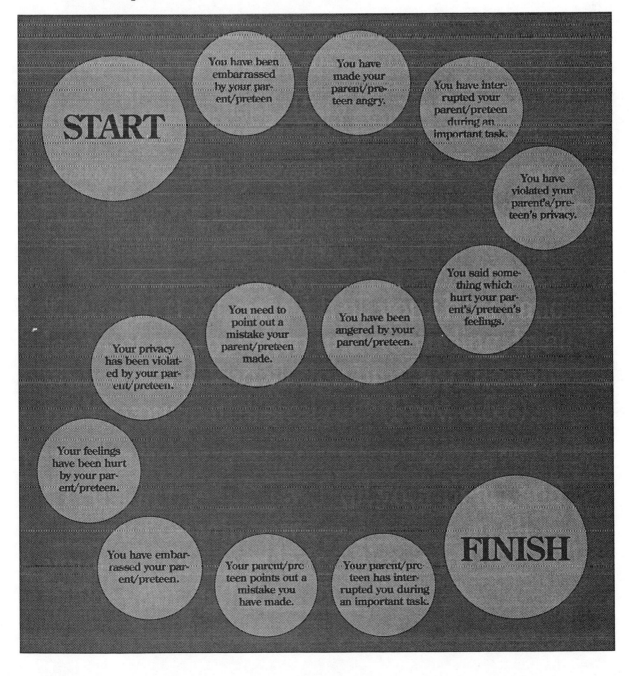

2. *Straight Talk.* Read Ephesians 4:29 together. What does this verse mean to you in light of the game you have just played?

3. *Prayer.* Ask God to help you flavor your daily conversations with respect. Pray especially that mutual respect would govern your exchanges during disagreements.

There's Nobody Quite Like You*

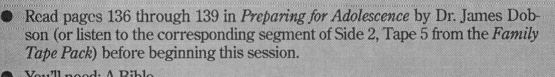

● Read pages 136 through 139 in *Preparing for Adolescence* by Dr. James Dobson (or listen to the corresponding segment of Side 2, Tape 5 from the *Family Tape Pack*) before beginning this session.

● You'll need: A Bible.

> Let me ask how well you are personally acquainted with yourself? Do you know who you are? Do you know what you want in life? Do you know your own strengths and weaknesses?
> *Preparing for Adolescence*, page 136

Discovering all the different dimensions of YOU doesn't happen overnight. In fact, it's a life-long project. Years from now, as you enter new phases—relationships, ministry, parenting—you will continue to discover new facets of YOU!

Sometime soon, ask your mom and/or dad to tell you about something new they've learned about themselves in the past year or so.

Self-discovery is a life-long adventure, and yours has just begun! Begin now to find new ways to expand your likes, talents and abilities. Experiment! Have fun! And most importantly, learn to appreciate the many things that make you unique in all the world.

> I urge you to shop around for who you are in the years that follow. Go out for various sports or try to learn to play a musical instrument....You might also go to the counseling office of your school and ask to be given some interest tests and vocational inventories that will identify your likes, dislikes, and skills. Joining the Scouts can also introduce you to many new dimensions of your personality. By all means, don't let these years slip by

without exploring the many possibilities that lie within you.
Preparing for Adolescence, page 137

*A 10 to 15 minute parent/preteen workout which complements Session 10 in the *Prepaging for Adolescence Group Guide*

The Activities

1. *I Am Unique.* Discover your uniqueness by answering the following questions:

Parent	Preteen
What is your favorite dessert?	
What is your hobby or favorite pastime?	
What do you most like to read?	
If you could visit any country in the world, which would you choose	
What is your favorite time to read the Bible and pray?	
Who is your best friend?	
What makes you happy?	
After Jesus, who is your favorite Bible character?	

2. *You Are Special.* Recognize each other's unique qualities by answering the following questions about each other. Talk about your comments as you write them:

Parent for Preteen	Preteen for Parent
What does he/she do better than most people?	
What is something you especially like about him/her?	
What is something good other people say about him/her?	
What is something about him/her that makes you smile?	
What is something about him/her that makes you feel proud?	

3. *A Work of Art.* Read Ephesians 2:10. Summarize the message of this verse in a simple drawing.

4. *Prayer.* Thank God that He has made you a unique creation. Ask Him to help you grow in confidence as His carefully crafted work of art.

Rejoice! You Belong to God!*

● Read pages 183 through 186 in *Preparing for Adolescence* by Dr. James Dobson before beginning this session (These last pages of the book are not recorded on an audiotape).

> There is a tendency during the adolescent years to feel that "today is forever"—that present circumstances will never change—that the problems you face at this moment will continue for the rest of your life....[However] if you find yourself unhappy for one reason or another during adolescence, just hang tough—things will change. That fact is one of life's certainties, and understanding it can help you cope with an uncomfortable circumstance.
> *Preparing for Adolescence*, page 183,184

In the coming years, every part of your life will be touched by change—your body, your emotions, your relationships with peers, your relationships at home.

In every possible arena, your identity will be shifted and shaped by the changing winds of adolescence.

If only there was something that would remain constant—just one thing that you could grasp for dear life through all the turbulence and adventure of the coming years...

I'm sure you know what I have in mind! Jesus Christ can be that one constant in your life. After all, He's the one who made you, and He knows better than anyone the best roads to take as you negotiate the path to adulthood!

Jesus Christ is the same yesterday and today and forever (Heb. 13:8).

*A 10 to 15 minute parent/preteen workout which complements Session 10 in the *Preparing for Adolescence Group Guide*.

The Activities

1. *Famous Last Words.* Take turns reading aloud chapter 7, "The Final Message" (pp. 183-186), in *Preparing for Adolescence.*

2. *Your Identity in Christ.* Your confidence and success as a Christian in your adolescent years is related to knowing who you are in Christ. The following statements summarize your identity in Christ. Read them aloud together:

I am the salt of the earth
(Matt. 5:13).

I am the light of the world
(Matt. 5:14).

I am a child of God
(John 1:12).

I am Christ's friend
(John 15:15).

I am chosen and appointed by Christ to bear His fruit
(John 15:16).

I am a slave of righteousness
(Rom. 6:18).

I am a joint heir with Christ, sharing His inheritance with Him
(Rom. 8:17).

I am a temple—a dwelling place—of God.
His Spirit and His life dwell in me
(1 Cor. 3:16; 6:19).

I am united to the Lord and am one spirit with Him
(1 Cor. 6:17).

I am a member of Christ's body
(1 Cor. 12:27; Eph. 5:30).

I am a new creation
(2 Cor. 5:17).

I am reconciled to God and am a minister of reconciliation
(2 Cor. 5:18,19).

I am a saint
(Eph. 1:1; 1 Cor. 1:2; Phil. 1:1; Col. 1:2).

I am God's workmanship—His handiwork—born
anew in Christ to do His work
(Eph. 2:10).

I am a fellow citizen with the rest of God's family
(Eph. 2:19).

I am righteous and holy
(Eph. 4:24).

I am a citizen of heaven
(Phil. 3:20; Eph. 2:6).

I am chosen of God, holy and dearly loved
(Col. 3:12; 1 Thess. 1:4).

I am a son of light and not of darkness
(1 Thess. 5:5).

I am a member of a chosen race, a royal priesthood,
a holy nation, a people for God's own possession
(1 Pet. 2:9,10).

I am an enemy of the devil
(1 Pet. 5:8).

I am a child of God and I will resemble Christ when He returns
(1 John 3:1,2).

I am born of God, and the evil one—the devil—cannot touch me
(1 John 5:18).

I am not the great "I AM" (Exod. 3:14; John 8:24,28,58),
but by the grace of God, I am what I am
(1 Cor. 15:10).[1]

3. *Your Growing Edge.* Each of you circle one statement you are most grateful for at this time in your life.

4. *Prayer.* Which one of the statements above reflects an area where your confidence in who you are needs to grow? Each of you circle that statement and pray together that God will increase your confidence in who you are in Christ.

1. Neil T. Anderson, adapted from his book *Victory Over the Darkness,* (Ventura, CA: Regal Books, 1990). Used by permission.